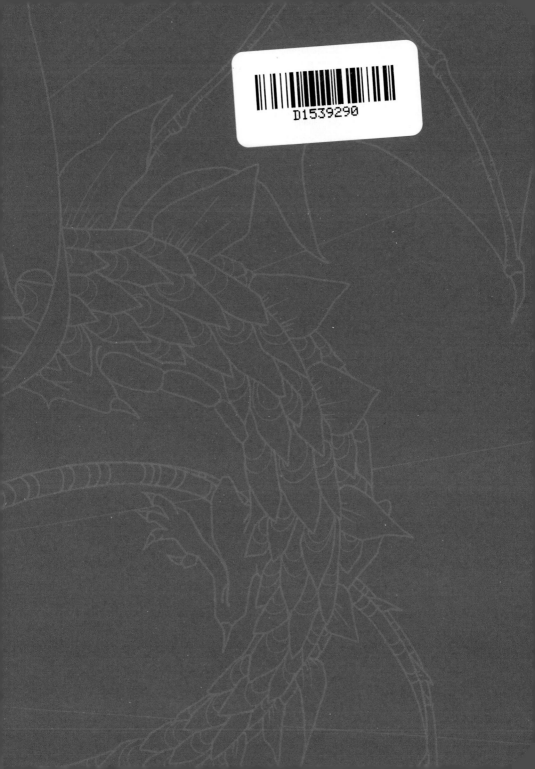

HOW TO DRAW
DRAGONS

*A Guide to Creating Fantastical Dragons
and the Realms They Inhabit*

BY JANE SULLIVAN

PETER PAUPER PRESS, INC.
WHITE PLAINS, NEW YORK

PETER PAUPER PRESS
Fine Books and Gifts Since 1928

OUR COMPANY

In 1928, at the age of twenty-two, Peter Beilenson began print-
ing books on a small press in the basement of his parents' home in
Larchmont, New York. Peter—and later, his wife, Edna—sought to
create fine books that sold at "prices even a pauper could afford."

Today, still family owned and operated, Peter Pauper Press continues
to honor our founders' legacy—and our customers' expectations—of
beauty, quality, and value.

Designed by Heather Zschock
Illustrations and text © 2016 Jane Sullivan

ISBN 978-1-4413-1979-1
Printed in China
7 6 5 4 3 2 1

INTRODUCTION

A.D. 793 —This year came dreadful fore-warnings over the land of the Northumbrians, terrifying the people most woefully: these were immense sheets of light rushing through the air, and whirlwinds, and fiery dragons flying across the firmament. –*from* The Anglo-Saxon Chronicle, *an eighth-century historical document*

But not all dragons are dreadful. Welcome to the wonderful world of dragons!

In this collection you will find dragons of all styles and breeds: fierce, playful, menacing, joyful, Celtic, Chinese, medieval, and more. Some live in caves, some reside underwater, some love mountains, some prefer forests, and some are themselves made of rocks or of flowers!

You'll see each dragon in this book evolve from a pencil sketch to a full-color beast, and learn how to create your own fiery creatures. The dragons begin with pencil drawings; progress to details in ink; and finally burst into living color. You'll learn to create dragons and fantasy designs in watercolor, gouache, colored pencil, and marker. Use the lightly outlined version of each dragon to get the hang of the linework and play with color. Then, try re-creating the dragon from start to finish on your own!

Many of the dragons in this book are drawn in styles and using techniques invented in the Middle Ages (when dragons, of course, still flew the skies and lurked in mountain caves). Layers of paint are added one over the other, and fine lines in opaque white are used to highlight and outline many parts of the design, just as in the detailed art of medieval illuminations. Of course, you may decide to adapt the guidance to your own preferred techniques, be they gouache or watercolor, pastels, oils, or acrylics. In the case of non-water-based media, you should also adjust your choice of painting surface: paper, card, board, or canvas.

Working in great detail will invite you to focus your attention on small areas of your work, and to pay attention to precision and delicacy at the tip of your pen or brush. In fact, beware! You will be drawn into the world of these marvelous creatures, and you may find yourself drifting further and further into the realm of the fantastic!

MATERIALS

Supplies for drawing dragons:

- **Drawing pencils**
- A **kneaded eraser**
- **Waterproof black ink pens:** either technical pens in a few line widths, or a traditional dip pen used with India or Chinese ink

Pencils are graded according to their softness. The softer the lead, the darker the shade, but also the more variation possible by pressing harder or more lightly as you work. In addition, a softer lead erases more easily when used with a light hand. I like to work with a **2B** or **3B** for the first step or two ("B" stands for "black," and this is the softer lead, ranging from **2B** to **8B**, which is very soft indeed). For more precision, I like a **B** or **HB**, the latter of which is the lead between the two grades ("H" stands for "hard lead"). Avoid the H range for your sketching and rough pencil work, as it is very difficult to erase; even a 2H is quite permanent!

Most of the dragons in this book are painted with **gouache**, a kind of opaque watercolor. To use gouache, put just a little into your palette at a time (though even when dry, it can be re-diluted with water). Gouache dries quite quickly, so though you will work in several layers of color, the waiting time between coats of paint can be as short as 15 to 30 minutes. It is a concentrated paint, so as you work you can add a few drops of water to the edge of the paint and pull it out with a wet brush, creating the consistency that you desire.

Always paint with the tip of the brush, never leaning heavily on the bristles, and never leave a brush standing in water, as the point will deform.

Supplies for working in gouache:

- A set of **artists' quality gouache paints**
- Good quality **brushes** in two or three sizes
- A **palette** for squeezing out your paint and for mixing
- A **cup of water** for cleaning your brush

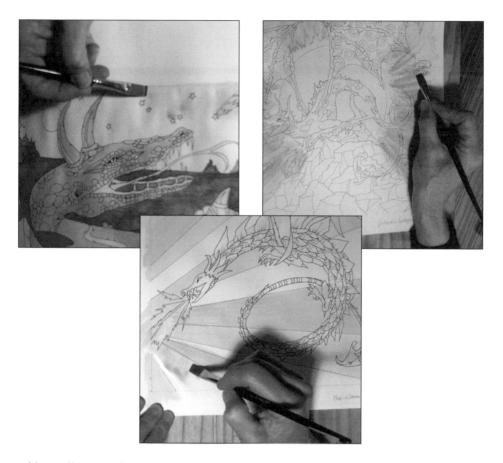

Additionally, some dragons use colored pencil or marker. These are a good starting point for learning about color and precision.

To work in colored pencil, select a set of soft pencils that lay down bright color without hard pressure. You can use water-based or alcohol-based markers, but choose blendable markers intended for illustration, in a range of colors beyond the primary.

If you take your dragon drawing adventures beyond the pages of this book, use heavy-weight drawing paper, watercolor paper (thick, so it won't buckle), Bristol board, or thick card. Avoid paper that is too textured, as it will be harder to draw and paint fine detail, and also avoid paper that is too shiny or has a finish that is "brilliant" or slippery.

COLOR THEORY

All colors of paint can be mixed to invent hundreds of different tones and nuances. Choose **zinc white** to mix with any color to create a paler shade, but use **permanent white** for pure white areas, or where using a fine brush to add highlights and outlines. The primary colors (blue, red, and yellow) are the basis for mixing the secondary shades of green, purple, and orange. Use the color wheel below as a reference for color mixing. This will also help you to identify the **complementary color** for each.

A primary color's complement is the color opposite on the wheel, the color obtained by mixing the other two primaries together. The complement of red is green, that of yellow is purple, etc. These two colors used next to one another can create a striking effect! Keep the complement of a color in mind as you paint, and use it sparingly to give zest and tension to your work.

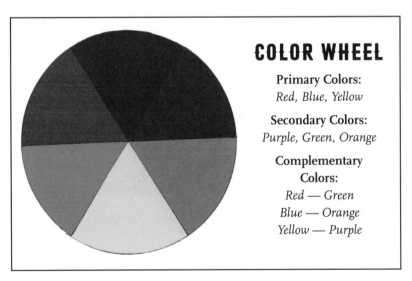

COLOR WHEEL

Primary Colors:
Red, Blue, Yellow

Secondary Colors:
Purple, Green, Orange

Complementary Colors:
Red — Green
Blue — Orange
Yellow — Purple

The colors are already chosen in the dragon drawings ahead, but feel free to experiment with your own original combinations of colors and nuances. The advantage of working with gouache is that it is opaque: if your color choice is not successful, you can always paint over with another color when dry!

COMPOSITION

You will see, in the early stages of each dragon, how important the composition of the page can be. When faced with a white page, begin by visualizing the overall movement or shape of the image. There are many ways to break up the space of the page: with a diagonal movement; with elements that suggest a triangle, pyramid, or circle; or with a sweeping curve or S-shape. Most of the dragons are based on a simple form that occupies the space and guides the eye to key features or encourages the viewer to make a complete "tour" of all the important elements in the picture. If there is no underlying form you risk ending up with a painting that seems confusing, rigid, or stagnant, and the viewer is quickly bored because the eye has no direction to follow.

KEY DRAGON FEATURES

Dragons come in all shapes and sizes, but most have a few things in common: claws and teeth, wings and scales. Here is a simplified guide to dragon features. Look at several of the dragons to see how they have been adapted to various situations and dragon bodies.

DRAGON HEAD IN FIVE STEPS:

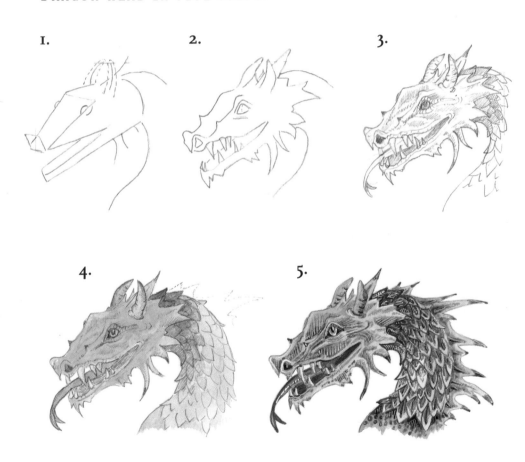

1.

2.

3.

4.

5.

DRAGON WING STYLES—FOUR EXAMPLES:

1.

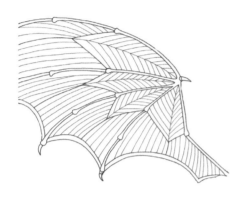

2.

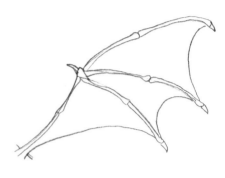

3.

4.

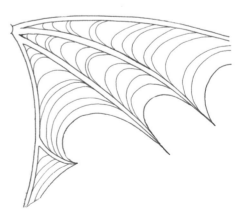

FOUR STYLES OF DRAGON EYES:

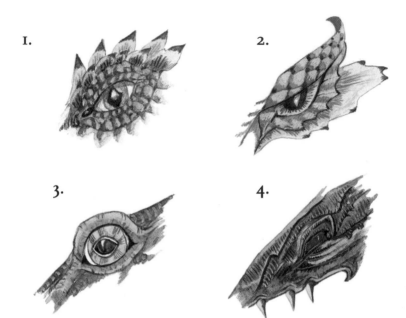

1.

2.

3.

4.

DRAGON CLAWS IN FOUR STEPS:

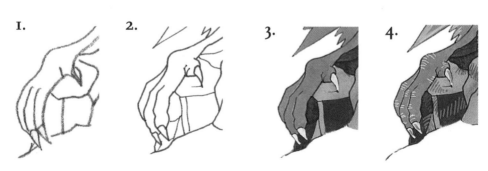

1.

2.

3.

4.

SPECIAL TECHNIQUES

In two of these dragons you will encounter Celtic knotwork, and the technique for creating these overs-and-unders of interlaced cords is quite simple. Here is a guide to making a rectangular knot.

HOW TO MAKE A KNOTWORK PANEL:

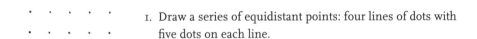

1. Draw a series of equidistant points: four lines of dots with five dots on each line.

2. In the center of each square formed by four points, make a small red dot. Visualize that each group of two black and two red dots creates a field or space in a diamond shape. (This does NOT need to be drawn, just imagined.)

3. For each diamond-shaped space (two black and two red dots), draw a section of diagonal cord that does NOT touch the dots. All adjacent cords must alternate from right to left diagonals. Do not draw cords where there are only THREE dots.

4. On the sides of the panel, where the three-dot spaces occur, fill in arches that connect the cords. At the four corners, the arches should touch the corner-dots to form spatula shapes.

5. The options for coloring these panels are endless. Often the background is filled in with black (which handily covers the dots!). Cords are usually painted in two or more colors, sometimes with highlighted lines that follow the curves in single or double lines.

PENCIL:

Begin with the central "S" that extends from the tip of the dragon's nose and sweeps down to his back. Keep the curve smooth. Add the horns, the head, and the neck. Next, indicate the placement of the wings. Finally, lay in the basic structure of the background: horizon line, mountains, and hills.

Once you are happy with the movement of the composition, you can begin to develop the character of the dragon. I like to begin this step with the eye, as it gives me a feeling for the personality of the creature! Continue with the body outline: the form of the mouth, a rough and rugged outline for the head, the points on the back-crest, and the anatomy of the wings.

Still working in pencil, and erasing and redefining from time to time, indicate the shape of the scales on the dragon's body, the volcano, the moon, and the trees and winding pathway on the hillside.

PEN AND INK:

When I put ink to paper, I often still have some details to add. You can complete these in the last pencil step, of course. But once you have figured out where you are going with scales and landscape, you often feel confident enough to complete the details with ink. This can be done with a fine-tip technical pen, or with traditional pen-and-ink (a pointed nib and good quality Chinese or India ink). When all the composition is established in ink, and dry, carefully erase all the pencil lines still visible.

GOUACHE:

Choose some of the principal areas of the design and apply washes of color. To do this, moisten an area with a paintbrush dipped in water and then, while the paper is still wet, lightly paint with watercolor or gouache. The paint will spread easily over the moistened area and create a light base of color. I use a wide, flat brush for the sky, and a pale coat of cobalt or cerulean blue. You may find that the paint creates accidental effects on wet paper, some areas darker than others or patterns that appear of their own accord. These textures may add interest to your design. If not, don't worry. Gouache is an opaque paint, and you can modify subsequently!

As you begin to fill in areas of the composition, you might change your mind about the season, color scheme, or time of day. Here, as I continued to paint with the greens and reds that I had chosen, I found that I wanted my dragon to be in a night-time setting. The pale blue sky became deeper blue, bringing intensity to the dragon head set against it. Blue and orange are complementary colors (see page 6), so the blue sky and russet orange dragon stand out vividly.

Some areas can be painted by using two or three colors and blending them together with a wet brush, as in the smoke from the volcano. Other colors can be made slightly bolder by repainting over the original light wash (a second coat will flow more evenly, and be smoother, than the first).

In the final step, use small brushstrokes of darker or lighter color to give texture and detail to all parts of the painting. On the ocean, darker blue and opaque white gouache suggest movement and variation; on the dragon's wings, lines of red are added and on his back-crest orange and white, while on the scales a yellow ochre gives contrast, and on the trees yellow and white suggest leaves.

White gouache will make the whole composition sparkle and to give definition to all the elements of the image. Use a very fine, pointed brush and keep the gouache not too runny.

Experiment with inking and coloring the lineart, then create your own rendition on the opposite page!

PENCIL:

In this composition, the basic movement is a loop that should be positioned harmoniously in the center of your page. Leave generous margins of white around the form, to allow for wings and background. I start with a single line to indicate the spiral along the top of the dragon's back and down to his tail, then I add the line that will define the shape of his head, body, and diminishing tail thickness.

The wings are positioned next, and they pass beyond the frame (although it's good to roughly draw both wings on scrap paper to see exactly how the anatomy of the wings works).

Now add the eye of the beast and some more of the body features, such as the scales standing up along the back, the legs and toes, the teeth, and the direction of the fire he is breathing out! Give the triangular tip of the tail an effect of three-dimensionality by turning the points to show their underside.

In the final pencil step, establish the anatomy of the wing bones and claws, and add the body scales.

PEN & INK:

When you arrive at the ink stage, work with a very fine-tip pen or nib to develop the character of the scales, the jagged edges of the flames from the mouth, and the rays of light (drawn with a ruler) behind the dragon. Don't forget to erase all the pencil lines once the ink has dried.

GOUACHE:

Begin with the rays of warm color behind the dragon, applying washes with a wide brush. Paint each area in turn first in clear water, then touch the wet surface with a little of the color desired and spread it quickly along the space, allowing some regions to remain slightly darker than others. Use a smaller brush to indicate the sprays of orange, red, or pink around the mouth-flames.

Now paint the first layer of color for the body, using a small or medium brush with a precise point. Work one color at a time, allowing each the time to dry before painting neighboring areas, so that the colors do not run into each other. Two colors are used for the mouth flames, blending the darker red close to the mouth with a rich orange farther out.

With white gouache, add the indispensable fine lines that bring to life each part of the dragon. A little shadow of darker ochre is also added on the wing bones, and the lighter green scales receive a touch of dark green to contrast with their darker green counterparts.

Experiment with inking and coloring the lineart, then create your own rendition on the opposite page!

GALACTIC DRAGON

PENCIL:

In setting up the composition of this scene, notice how there are two triangular forms, one super-imposed on the other: the rock is similar to a pyramid and the space between the two wings above is like a smaller "V." Echoing this theme, the wings are divided into three triangles each. Between these two triangles (rock and negative space between the wings), the dragon himself follows a gentle swirl of rounded lines from the skull, along the neck and back, and looping down the tail. I've already added the eye at this stage, just to get a feeling for the creature's personality!

Now work up the wing structure, and add the markings on the drag-on's body, his toes and claws, teeth and back scales.

Here you can develop the rock surface, with a variety of planes suggesting different facets. Place the sun behind the creature, and other planets around him. He may not be exactly "fire-breathing," as there's no air for fire in space, but some sort of beam is escaping his mouth...

PEN & INK:

When you arrive at the ink stage, you are ready to decorate the wings and even the planets.

GOUACHE:

Three color washes are put in place in this step. The sun and rock are perhaps the simplest (the sun wash can even pass through the dragon, as the light yellow will be covered by the body color in the next step). For the more complicated sky wash, begin with a fairly wet wash of pale blue, and while it's still wet, add more concentrated paint (the same color) using the tip of a medium brush, or even the corner of a wide brush (if you used one for the basic wash).

Now use richer colors to paint the first layer of the main features: dragon, rock, and planets. Notice that the dragon contains a rich purple that contrasts nicely with the yellows behind, exploiting the effect on the eye of complementary colors (see page 6).

Contrasting colors on the first layer, fine white lines, and even a touch of gold marker on the star-rays if desired complete this outer-space monster.

Experiment with inking and coloring the lineart, then create your own rendition on the opposite page!

PENCIL:

Begin by drawing a horizon line with a ruler, and placing the circles for the setting sun (using a compass if needed), just off-center. Then place the sweeping, gently waving line of the dragon's back, and finally add the position of the head, eye, tongue, under-body, leaf-shaped tail, and wing bones.

Next, work on the dragon's body, elaborating the wing structure, body scales, face, legs, and feet. Notice how the left wing turns at the end to suggest a little spatial depth, and how the scales begin at the neck, to be continued in an overlaying pattern all down the body when you reach the pen and ink stage.

In the final pencil step, add the details of the sea and mountains over which the dragon soars.

PEN & INK:

This step contains a lot of detail, and can be done first in pencil if you wish. If you feel confident enough, however, you can add the slopes of the mountains, construct the island castle, and fill in the lines on the dragon's wings in a spider-web motif using a fine black pen. I couldn't help adding a little sea monster taking his evening swim in the sunset waters!

GOUACHE:

The first colors to lay in are those done with washes of gouache on already damp areas: the sun rays, the sea, and the mountains (allowing the paint to suggest a variety of tones and variations in dark and light). To follow, I start painting the sun, the castle, and the details of the sea, the serpent, and the little Viking-style sailboat.

Now the colors of the landscape and sea can be enriched with a second layer of slightly contrasting colors, and the basic tones of the dragon can be added.

The final step, as usual, is where the white gouache comes into play, with fine lines that follow the contours of sea currents, mountain slopes, dragon scales, wing bones, feet, and claws. Even the turrets of the castle will shine and sparkle when they have a little touch of opaque white added!

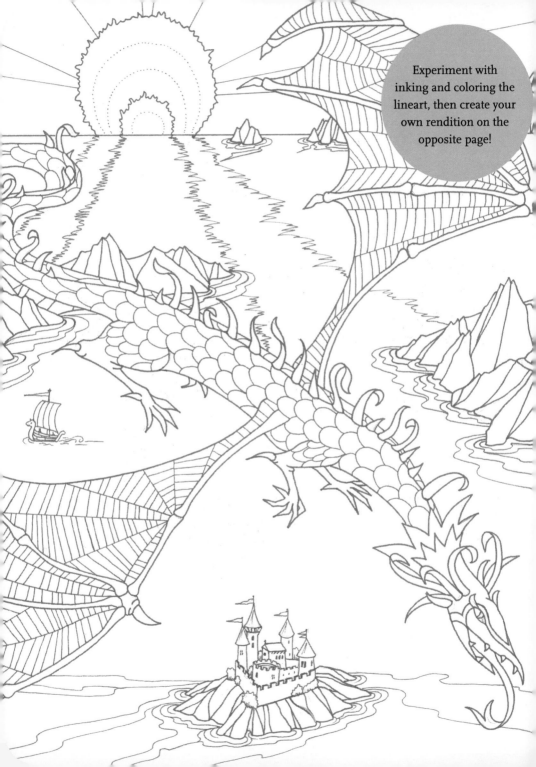

Experiment with inking and coloring the lineart, then create your own rendition on the opposite page!

PENCIL:

The two main characters of this scene are the first part of the composition to position. The creature's head is the focal point, so that is drawn (without too much detail) in the middle of the page. Then visualize the movement of the sea dragon's body in its receding arches, and indicate these very roughly with single pencil lines that are then doubled. Then add a third line, which will be where the scales along the crest will be placed. Then add the mermaid. Notice how the line of the dragon's head is continued in the diagonal of the mermaid's extended arm, and even her finger, which is swirling circles in the water!

Now the secondary elements can be drawn in: pinnacle rocks, a crescent moon, and two friendly fishes listening in on the conversation. (Undoubtedly, the problem for the monster lies in the annoying fact that he has a knot in his tail!)

Details on the two characters can be drawn in now, and suggestions for the movement of color on the surface of the water as well.

PEN & INK:

With your ink (which could be black, or even blue or sea green in fact), continue to add detail to the bodies and tails of the creatures, and intricacy to the rocks and sea. The belly of the sea-dragon is given a slightly rounded effect at the angle of each horizontal line, just bulging out a bit here and there. The horizon line in the background is inked with a ruler.

GOUACHE:

The first colors are those of the sky and sea, which establish the palette for this area: royal and pale blues and sea-greens. The moon leaves a bright yellow reflection on the distant water.

To complement the yellow of the moonlight, I chose a palette of purples and pinks for my monster and for the mermaid's tail, with a little touch of sea-green and seaweed-red as well. The mermaid's hair and the fins of one of the fishes echo the yellow of the moonlight, and lead the eye of the viewer around the scene and back into the neck and head of the central character.

The addition of the white gouache softens the initial strong, flat effect of all the colors, and highlights the shimmering quality of the moonlit setting.

Experiment with inking and coloring the lineart, then create your own rendition on the opposite page!

PENCIL:

Even though you know that the dragon will be partially hidden by trees, you need to position his whole body first, to have all the visible parts in the right places. Keep the pencil lines very light, so you can easily erase those that will be behind the trees. Sketch the form of the knight on his charger, making sure that the dragon has him well in his sights! Note how the sweep of the neck, back, and tail make one continuous and fluid line of movement.

Now you can add the forest, beginning with the trees right in front of the dragon and the tree trunk that is held by her right forepaw. The tops of the trees behind her also cover parts of her tail, giving a feeling of depth to the composition.

Place the foreground rocks off center, and add the pathway, grasses, and a little more detail on the knight.

PEN & INK:

As usual, I add more detail to the dragon's body and the knight at this stage of ink-work, but you can also do this work in pencil before inking. I drew little faces on the tree trunks....but this is, of course, optional!

GOUACHE:

In this step you can see two or three layers of color on the grass and trees: an initial base color, a second layer with blades of grass (done with the point of the brush) and leaves (done by lightly pressing the hairs of the brush onto the paper), and in the case of the grass, a second layer of yellow grasses on top of the first green ones. A base color is also painted onto the sky and the pathway.

The same techniques continue here, building up the density of the grass, and adding base colors and then leaves to the trees. A small sponge is used to make the clouds: slightly dilute a little white gouache in a shallow bowl and dip the sponge in, then pat it lightly onto the blue base color of the sky.

The trees continue to be painted in the same way, with autumnal colors, and the rocks take on a blue tint, while a bluebird perches in one of the trees. I also began to think that a little blue should be used in the dragon's body, to complement the orangey reds in some of the trees.

Use the same tone of red-orange for the claws and tongue of the dragon and for a few details on the knight, thus offering the eye a link between the two characters. Continue to add richly colored leaves to the trees.

Here you see the dragon and knight fully painted, using the techniques in the preceding projects: a solid color that receives a second partial coat of the same tone a little darker to suggest form and shadow, and then the fine lines of white to outline and highlight.

Experiment with inking and coloring the lineart, then create your own rendition on the opposite page!

PENCIL:

Position the central diamond-shape first, and the surrounding motifs of butterfly, sun, snails, and peaceful landscape.

Consider the space of the diamond your composition area, and arrange the harmonious curve of the little dragon, his wing placement, the soft petals of the flowers, and the fluid curves of the stems. Notice that there are no straight lines inside the diamond. The eye is peacefully guided around the different parts of the layout with no abrupt changes of direction. The little dragon's gaze is concentrated on the butterfly, of course.

Add detail to the leaf-like wings and the leafy motifs on the body, and add the other plant forms to balance the image.

PEN & INK:

Use the ink step to help make the little dragon stand out from his busy background of lines by outlining him with a medium-tip pen. Using a fine-tip pen, add the veins on the leaves, the tiny flowers, the detail on the petals, and then the other details elsewhere on the exterior motifs and landscape.

GOUACHE:

Apply very light color washes to the background. Moisten the area with clear water first, so that when you add your touches of blue, yellow, and pink, they can be blended gently to run one into the other.

I began by laying in the base colors of the background first, but you can also begin with the central part of the painting. The earthy colors of the snails are echoed in the butterfly, to accentuate the diagonal already established by the general direction of the dragon's body and his regard fixed on the butterfly.

The little dragon is painted in pastel purples, all mixed from the same two colors (purple being a blend of red, or crimson, and blue) with variations in the addition of more or less red or blue, or with the addition of a little zinc white. The same colors are used for the diamond frame. Continue to lay in all the other base colors, giving the flower the same hues as the snails and butterfly, to reinforce the diagonal tension already indicated. Pale blues and pinks are used on the small flowers so as not to weigh too heavily on the eye.

And the final step, as usual, is the addition of fine white lines and even dots, to soften the force of solid areas of color, and to add sparkle and definition.

Experiment with inking and coloring the lineart, then create your own rendition on the opposite page!

PENCIL:

A graceful S-curve is established in the first pencil step for this dragon. At this stage you can also put the wings in place. Notice how the foreground wing is larger, as it's closer to the viewer, and how the background wing appears slightly turned. Where the wings leave the dragon's back, they form a "V," intersected by the creature's curving neck. Keep the head lifted, to give a feeling of upward movement and a regal posture.

Continue with the anatomy of the wings, adding the jointed bones and pointed decoration. Begin drawing the belly scales and the head, and add the legs and claws.

Now that the dragon occupies his place in the composition, you can add the waters and rocky shores below the dragon, as well as the distant mountains. Complete the pencil-work by drawing in the lines on the wings and the small scales on the dragon's body.

PEN & INK:

With your fine-tip pen, redraw all the pencil lines and add extra indications of light on the mountains, bushes, trees, and currents in the water. Erase all the pencil before painting.

GOUACHE:

Choose a shade of blue that pleases you (I like Prussian blue, but you may prefer ultramarine, cobalt, turquoise, or cerulean), and use the same color for a light wash across the sky and a darker effect in the water. Using the same hue will give unity and harmony to the overall painting.

Add a different blue that contrasts with the first, and select a range of other colors as the background's base hues.

Begin painting the dragon, using some of the same colors found in the background. Too many different hues can create a chaotic sensation; limit your palette so that the painting hangs together with dynamic, but not confusing, energy!

In fact, all of the colors used for the dragon appear also in the background, except the vibrant red that is reserved for the beast alone. Some of the shared colors are, however, more solid and flat on the dragon than in the water, for example.

The stage of applying white detail lines is a fun moment in this painting, as this is a dragon with particularly fashionable wing decoration! You could even continue adding more intricate designs to his wings or scales. The possibilities are endless.

Experiment with inking and coloring the lineart, then create your own rendition on the opposite page!

DRAGON ROCK

PENCIL:

This painting has a special creative origin, because it comes from an image of a beautiful rock in the sea near the island of Corsica. Using the outline of the huge rock, I transformed the top section into a dragon-form, as if he had grown out of the rock itself. Therefore, the basic form of this composition is not, perhaps, as flowing as others, but it remains somewhat harmonious with the rock shape below it.

When the wing and back crest are added, and some of the smaller rock shapes, the mass of the dragon-rock begins to come together. Now you can also add the outlines of the background mountains.

Continue building up the dragon with scales, wings, and head detail, and add more lines to the rock. To contrast with the rigidity of the rocks, a flowing strip of ocean is added in the foreground.

PEN & INK:

As previously noted, you can add all the detail given in the ink step when you are still working with pencil, and then ink over the same lines. But with practice, you will probably find that you can draw in more and more detail directly with your pen.

GOUACHE:

Two different tones of blue are used for the initial washes of water in the central space and in the foreground. Yellows and pinks are used in washes for the rays of the rising sun behind the mountains.

Russet orange alternates with the browns of the stone to make this a fantastical and living rock! A coat of white gouache is laid onto the snow-topped mountains, and while still wet, a hint of blue is added on the left side of each peak.

This magical rock inspires more and more fantasy in color-choice! Shades of purple and blue are used on the dragon's scales and the foreground folly of fishes is painted in tones already found in the main section of the image.

White gouache adds the sparkle of light to all parts of the painting and defines the angles of some of the rock formation as well. Ink lines between the sun-rays are covered by white also, to link the colors more subtly.

Experiment with inking and coloring the lineart, then create your own rendition on the opposite page!

CELTIC DRAGON

PENCIL:

Begin by positioning the panel of knotwork (see page 11) in a long rectangle along the bottom of the page. The body of the dragon is then placed almost in the center, just enough to the left to leave space for the wings. Sketch in the form of the head with its teardrop-shaped eye, and the directions for each of the legs. The tail will loop through the knotwork, so you can roughly indicate its shape.

Fill in the panel of Celtic interlace using the instructions on page 11. Complete the form of the wings and draw in the legs, which have a traditionally Celtic look. Now begin adding loops of knots in the remaining spaces, just using a continuous pencil line and not worrying (yet!) about establishing the "overs and unders."

PEN & INK:

All that you see here should be drawn carefully in pencil before going over each line again in fine-tip marker or ink. All of the background knots must be sketched first in single lines, then doubled. Finally, you will need to use a small or pointed eraser to adjust all the intersections of cords, so that they alternate between "over" and "under."

When the panel of interlace at the bottom of the page is completed in pencil, loop the dragon's tail through several of the knots. Fill her wings with spirals and petal forms, as found in medieval Irish and Anglo-Saxon art. Trace over your pencil lines in ink, and then erase the pencil.

MARKER:

Begin by coloring the dragon her-self, so that you can keep his form clearly defined as you fill in other colors around her.

You will need fine-tipped markers for this detailed design. Balance the two or three colors you choose evenly across the page. Add dots, spirals, and swirls to the dragon's body using a darker color on top of the base color.

Color the knotwork panel to highlight the heart-shaped knots in red, with orange and yellow for the rest. Filling in between the cords will cover any remaining dots left from your layout technique for this style of interlace. Decorate the cords with a second color on top of the first, to further complicate matters!

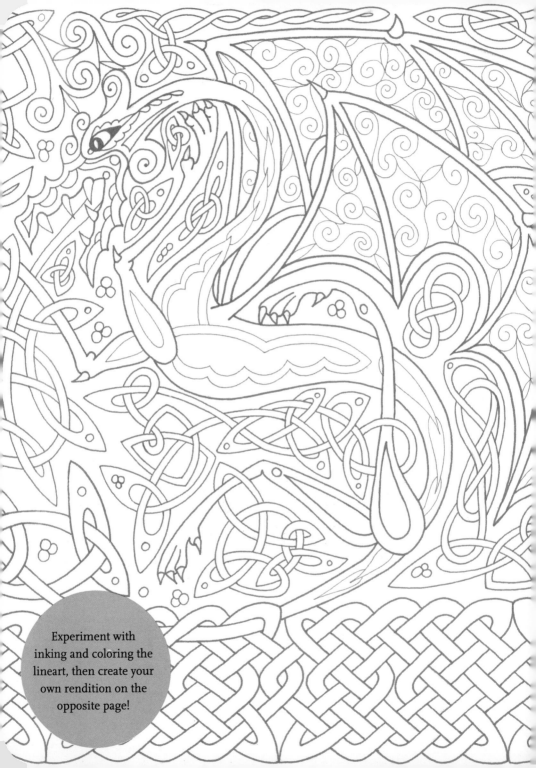

Experiment with
inking and coloring the
lineart, then create your
own rendition on the
opposite page!

PENCIL:

Often in the illuminated manuscripts of the Middle Ages, one finds fantastic creatures cavorting in the margins, sometimes even around a very serious or sacred text! Here we zoom in on the corner of an imaginary page to witness a scene of manuscript madness.

Begin by positioning the corner lines (bottom and right-hand side) with their little hearts and swirling hook, leaving ample space outside of these lines for the other designs to come.

Inside the space, sketch your dragon with his triple tail, each ending in another head.

Now who is looking at whom?! Add a bit more detail to the main dragon, face to face with one of the tail-heads, and on a branch at top right place a dancing owl, who exchanges a glance with another of the tails. Below on the bottom line is a skinny greyhound, a stylized unicorn, a fat cat, and an ordinary dog-snail (?!), who deserves the amused look of the final tail-head.

A friendly flying rabbit happens to be passing by overhead, and a giant ladybug crawls up the vertical line at right.

Manuscripts are complex and over-populated places! The early scribes had a horror of empty spaces, or just loved (as I do) filling in these inviting areas with curling vines, flowers, and leaves. Keep the lines fluid and graceful, often alternating the direction of curves: one to the right, one to the left, etc.

PEN & INK:

When you come to ink all this nonsense, pull out all the stops— flowers with faces, musician mice, butterflies made of hearts, leaves of unknown species that twist and turn, and even a pretty bow on the tail of the cat! Look at negative spaces, and fill them with movement and interest. On the original two lines, place half-circles and curved motifs where you can later add a touch of gold.

GOUACHE:

Begin the color stage by deciding on the nuances for the dragon. Lay in the first, bold colors in flat coats of gouache.

Use a different palette of colors for the rest of the scene, but retain the rich red as a unifying element and distribute it fairly evenly over other parts of the decoration.

Highlight details across the image with white gouache to bring it all to life.

I remembered having seen, in a 13th-century manuscript in the north of France, a very charming red unicorn, and he haunted me! I couldn't help myself: I had to paint the unicorn red.

Experiment with inking and coloring the lineart, then create your own rendition on the opposite page!

PENCIL:

Position this dragon of good luck so that he fills the page with well-rounded curves. Notice how the splayed tail and the placement of the horns seem to close the circular movement, so that the eye will continue to turn around the whole picture, accentuating the rolling and looping impetus of this friendly sea monster.

In the following steps you can begin to create the character of the dragon, and also to add the spirals of the stylized waves. No straight lines permitted!

PEN & INK:

As previously mentioned for other dragons, you can draw in all the detail in one of the pencil steps, rather than waiting until you redraw in ink. Here you see the scales, fancy head adornment, and concentric lines of the waves all in place.

GOUACHE:

The palette chosen for this dragon is mainly blue, but with some apple green, pale yellow, purples, and pinks as well. Begin with some light color washes on body and sea, then lay in some of the flat color areas.

In the spirals of the waves, paint a darker blue band over the background wash of light blue (the same color in fact, only the first coat was very diluted). In the same way, darker shades of the colors elsewhere are also added: green on green, blue on blue, and even blue on light green.

Complete the coloring with the addition of white lines and dots.

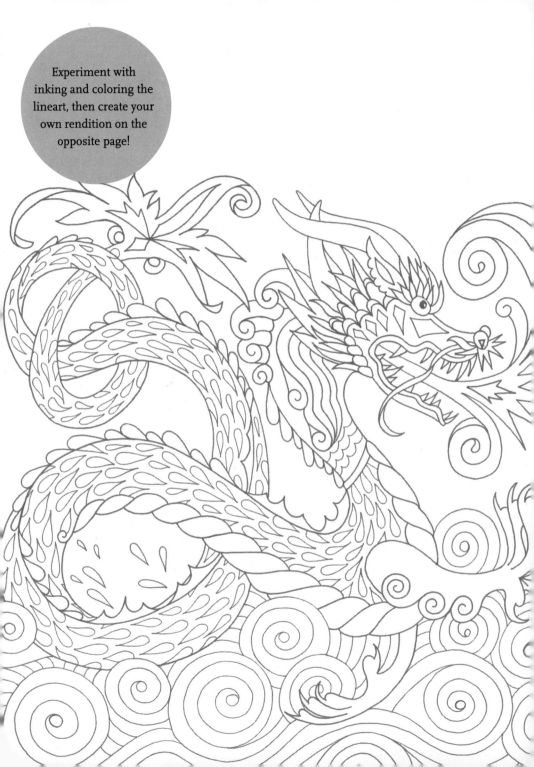

Experiment with inking and coloring the lineart, then create your own rendition on the opposite page!

DRAGONFLY DRAGON

PENCIL:

Establish the diagonal direction of the body, and then position the wings and head. Fill most of the page with the dragon, but leave a margin all around for the other elements of the painting.

Begin filling in the background with the curve of the pond's shore, some water lilies and lily pads, and two frogs. Add detail to the dragon's head and begin filling in the veins on his wings.

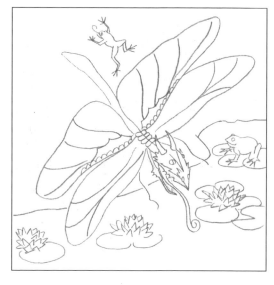

PEN & INK:

Continue to fill the scene with grasses, cattails, and ripples in the water. The wings of the dragonfly are complex, with a mixture of markings. You might choose to draw all the detail in pencil first, before inking, and then maybe use a slightly thicker marker or pen to ink the dragon himself, to help him to stand out from his detailed background.

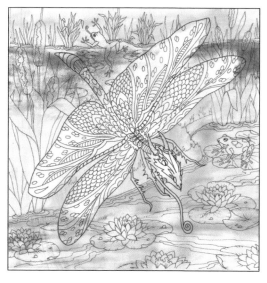

GOUACHE:

Paint the washes depicted from top to bottom, moistening the section of the paper you're working on with clear water, then adding your wash of green or blue. Allow each to dry before doing the next, so that they don't overlap and run into each other.

Use several different greens for the lily pads and grasses, and a bold medium blue for some of the ripples on the water's surface.

Rich red and bright yellow in the cattails contrast with a delicate palette of pinks and mauves for the flowers. Continue painting the greens of grasses and leaves, and give the frog and toad their first layer of color too.

For our fantastical insect-dragon, create a combination of magenta, smoky blue, lemon yellow, and sunny orange that flashes across the page!

Bring the scene to detailed life with fine lines and dots of white gouache on the dragonfly, yellow veins on the leaves, and extra shading on grasses and lily pads.

Experiment with inking and coloring the lineart, then create your own rendition on the opposite page!

PENCIL:

Use the curve of the dragon's body to divide the space with a diagonal, almost "yin-yang" movement. Position the wings of the dragon, and then the softly rounded back, neck, and belly of the unicorn. Use his legs to frame one of the wings and also the dragon's head.

Add detail to both the dragon and the unicorn, balancing how the bodies of both occupy the open spaces without seeming cramped or uncomfortable. In fact, you want to give the impression that the two characters are turning in a counter-clockwise direction, around and around, almost as if dancing!

Indicate very roughly the motifs for each creature: butterflies or bats, flowers or hexagons.

PEN & INK:

With a fine-tip marker, or even with a pointed pen and gouache in appropriate colors, complete the line art and continue to add decoration to both bodies, plus extra exterior motifs of butterflies and lightning bolts.

Choose your base colors for each creature. Here I used pink for the unicorn and pale green for the dragon. Notice how the intensity of the colored pencil can be varied with pressure, giving the effect of shading and allowing room for darker details to be added later.

Here I stayed in the same color ranges for both animals, adding darker green (with lighter and heavier pressure) to the dragon and purple to the pinks of the unicorn.

Now add blue, and its complement orange, to the dragon's body, and orange to the unicorn. A few areas of orange on both creatures serve to unify the image.

Experiment with inking and coloring the lineart, then create your own rendition on the opposite page!

PENCIL:

In the center of your page, position the shield and helm. The horizontal top of the shield (drawn with a ruler) is about one-third of the way down from the top of the page. Leave plenty of room for the tattered stylized fabric of the banners or drapes to either side.

To construct the shield, draw two vertical lines descending from the ends of the horizontal, roughly one-third of the distance you envisage using for the whole shield. Place the point of a compass at the end of the right-hand vertical and, starting with the pencil point on the end of the opposite vertical, mark the bottom curve of the shield on that side. Repeat for the other side.

Historically, in heraldic art, the size of the helm was in proportion to that of the shield, as if they were part of a real suit of armor. Here, however, I have reduced the size of the helm, to allow plenty of room for a decorative little dragon atop it.

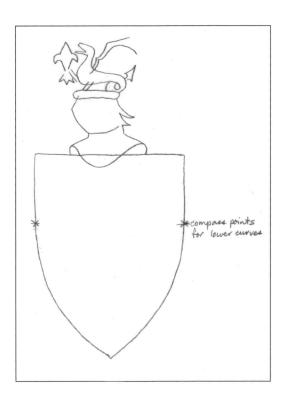

compass points for lower curves

Indicate quite roughly the position of the leaves that will frame the shield, and also draw the top line of the scroll that billows around the base of the shield. At every turn in the scroll, indicate the fold of the parchment going downwards.

Each central line that you have drawn is now transformed into leaf motifs that turn and twist. Fill the shield itself with its dragon motif, and complete the bottom line of the parchment scroll.

PEN & INK:

You may have finalized a lot of this detail in pencil before arriving at this step, but if not you can now add detail to the dragon and helm, and in Roman capitals you can write the motto "*Vexilla Draconum Prodeunt*" ("The Standards of the Dragons Advance") onto the scroll.

GOUACHE:

I chose regal colors for the coat of arms: gold and silver. Balance the two colors across the leaves and begin painting the dragon. The burnished gold and silver are done with markers here, but you can also use gouache (in tubes) or powdered gouache (such as TroCol bronze powders, which are also mixed with water and give an excellent metallic effect).

Other colors are now added to the dragon and helm decoration and to the scroll.

Finally, white gouache is used to highlight and outline throughout the image, and then the finishing touch is added: with a pointed nib and very pale blue gouache, encircle everything in a fine line, just a couple of millimeters from all the painted areas.

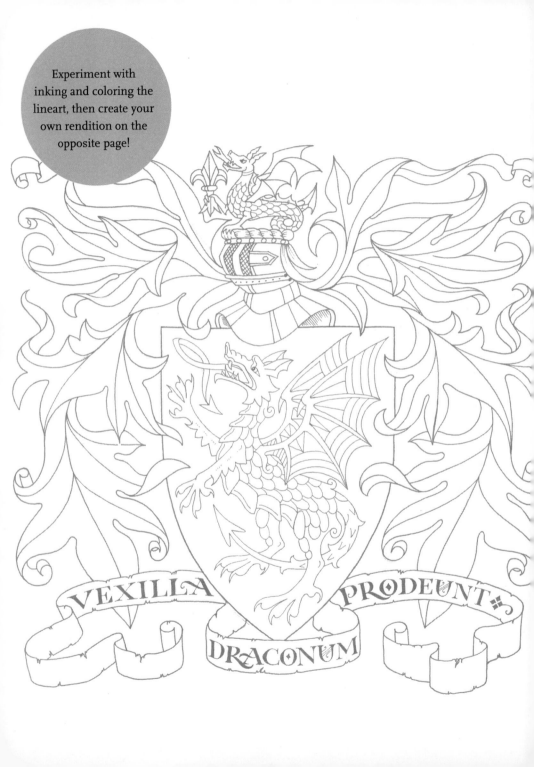

Experiment with inking and coloring the lineart, then create your own rendition on the opposite page!

VEXILLA PRODEUNT DRACONUM

CHINESE CLOUD DRAGON

PENCIL:

A nice "S" curve places this dragon's body in the center of the page. Add to this her head (a simple shape like a sideways "V") and the prolongation of her tail, ending in a little spiral.

With the addition of head features, legs with curving claws, and stylized clouds around her, the dragon immediately takes on a joyful personality! Don't forget her sacred pearl, floating just above her head.

PEN & INK:

The detail added in the ink step for this dragon is quite easy, so you may be able to do it directly in marker or pointed pen without too much pencil work beforehand. The scales are built up, starting from behind the dragon's head, in triangular or inverted "V" forms of various sizes, one on top of the other. The first cloud shapes are now joined by banks of concentric circles, and the pearl is given its petal-like rays of light. Erase all the pencil lines when you have the ink step completed.

MARKER:

Use fine-tip markers to color the dragon's body, alternating between two base colors to distribute them fairly evenly.

Now add some colors to make your dragon "flash"! You can vary colors within a single body part, such as the tongue.

Add restrained gray detail to the spiral-and-wave clouds and leave lots of white to shine through. Yellow, peach, and orange are used for the pearl's rays.

Add little dots and lines sparingly, using a metallic gold marker, for brilliance and sparkle!

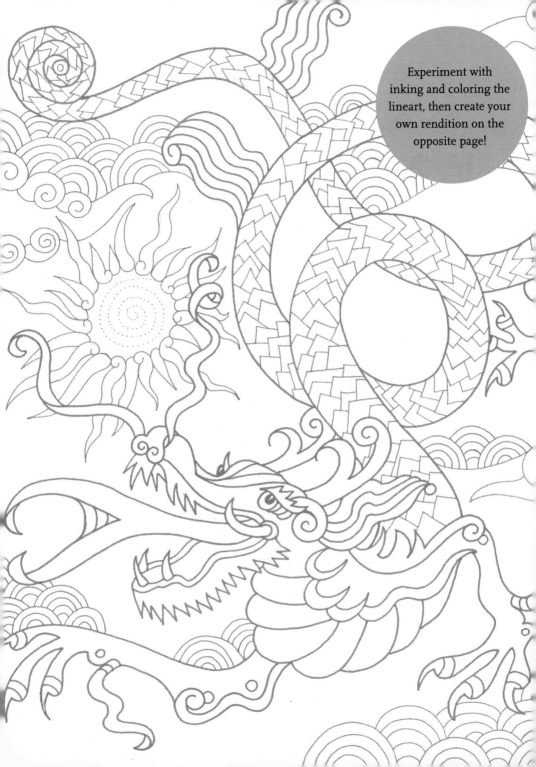

Experiment with inking and coloring the lineart, then create your own rendition on the opposite page!

FAT LIZARD LORD

PENCIL:

This little dragon was based on a photograph of a lizard taken in the tropics. His body has a curious shape, almost like a sweet potato! His bowed legs are indicated with little curving pencil lines, and his wings with fairly evenly balanced "S" curves. With his head in this position, you can see the inside of his roaring mouth.

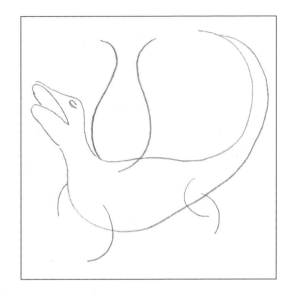

Draw the arched wings, which turn on themselves, and the basic forms of the flowers.

PEN & INK:

Now the fun begins! Fill in exotic petals, leaves, lilies, and ferny loops all around him, and then draw the parallel lines on his chevron-wings and tummy, and the strange beard under his upturned chin. Don't forget to erase your pencil work before beginning to paint.

GOUACHE:

With apple-green gouache, paint
the wings and make diamonds on
the body. After this, paint the body
in yellow, allowing the green of the
diamonds to run a little as the wet
yellow touches them. This creates
a nice texture, almost a shadow,
under the wings. Continue with a
medium blue and a smoky blue (a
mixture of turquoise and white).

Peach, pink, and purple are used
for the background, to contrast
with the greens and blues of the
lizard (who has, however, a nice red
tongue!).

Add some darker shading to parts of the wing and belly stripes, and to the back crest, then paint white gouache details everywhere you can—even in dozens of tiny dots around the central circles of the flowers!

Experiment with inking and coloring the lineart, then create your own rendition on the opposite page!

PENCIL:

Begin the layout of this composition with a central "V" shape. Then add the spiral of the dragon's back, doubled to make the body, and add to this the beak-like head (position the dragon's eyes high on this forehead). Draw the pointed arches of the wings.

Add to dragon's body detail a little more, and indicate the background trees and the lapping water at the shoreline in front of him.

PEN & INK:

With the main areas of the picture in place, you can begin to construct the creature's armor! Notice how the lines of body scales are notched and rough-edged. Work carefully on the eye, to capture the dragon's mistrustful personality! Add lines to the wings, a crest to the bending tail, leaves and shrubbery beyond and between the trees, and that rather sinister-looking bone protruding from the water's edge—the last remnant of lunch?

GOUACHE:

Begin with washes in blue and green on the forest, ochre on the sand, and pale blue for the water. Allow the paint, added to a wet surface, to find its own place and variations of intensity.

Continue by painting in the solid body colors on the dragon.

And now paint the trunks of the trees, the large tropical leaves in the forest, the smaller ones on the sand, and the various blues and greens of the water.

With your white gouache, highlight and outline as indicated, and add horizontal strokes to the dark tree trunks, darker patches on the reddish trees, and vertical strokes to the ochre ones to add texture to the wood colors. And, if you're not too squeamish, a little blood on the bone!

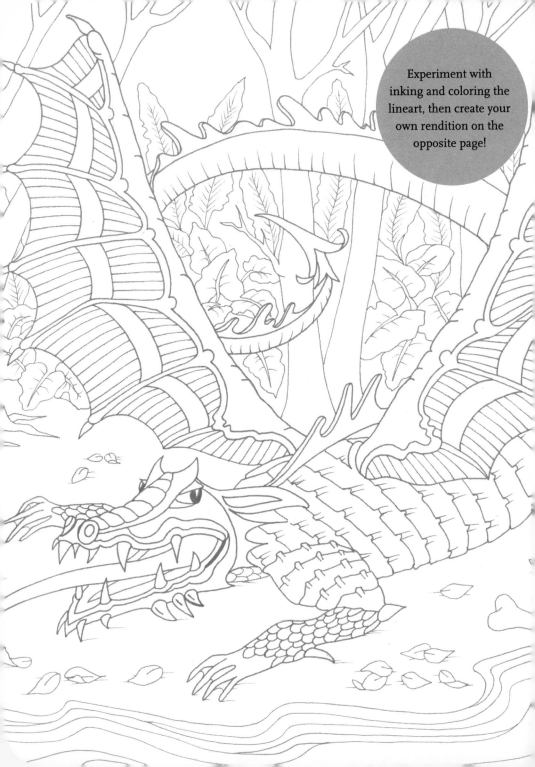

Experiment with inking and coloring the lineart, then create your own rendition on the opposite page!

PENCIL:

Begin with the sweeping curve of
the back, and then fill out the form
of the chest with a second curve.
Add the loop of the tail, very fluid
and graceful (ending in a triangular
arrowhead point), and the uplifted
head. Frame the head with the
principal wing bone lines, and then
suggest an overall circular shape
with the generous curves of the
wings themselves.

Next, establish the outlines of the
silhouette of the entire dragon.
Only when you have these pencil
lines satisfactorily in place can you
begin filling in with flowers and
leaves—right up to the edges of this
contour.

PEN & INK:

All the interior space of the dragon must be tightly packed with flowers—even the eye is a flower! Use petals or pointed leaves for the claws, and large expansive flowers on the wings. The tail ends in a beautiful bouquet!

MARKER:

Select your first color, using a very fine-tip marker, and distribute the hue here and there across the whole image.

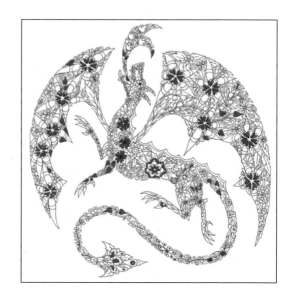

Two shades of green are added, used mostly for leaves and vines.

And finally, all the other colors are filled in, with secondary patches or lines of darker or contrasting colors laid on top of many of the petals. Don't forget the little touch of white left in the corner of the eye, to bring it to life!

Experiment with inking and coloring the lineart, then create your own rendition on the opposite page!

FIREBALL GAMES

PENCIL:

No need for a compass really, as there will be flames to cover the contour of the "ball," but position this central element of the design in the exact middle of your page. After this, sketch in the four young dragon heads, and then simply the swirls to indicate the movement of their bodies.

Now you can add to the anatomy of the dragons, their bodies, legs, and wings. Keep moving around the image, rather than working one at a time, so that you are sure to retain a harmonious mixture of line direction, points, angles, and curves.

PEN & INK:

You can draw in the details of wing structure, faces, feet and claws, and the flames on the ball in pencil first, before inking in all of your design. Erase well afterwards, so that stray pencil marks are not "trapped" under the first paint wash.

GOUACHE:

Moisten the entire page using a sponge or wide brush, and then, with a large soft brush, drag colors out from the central ball: yellows, oranges, and pinks. You can allow the wash to go right over the dragons; when painted, their colors will cover the wash.

You might begin by painting the fireball before the dragons, as you will have the colors already to hand in the palette you used for the background wash.

I selected one shade of green, a rich olive, to unite the body colors of all four of the sporty friends. Each one received a part of his coloration in this hue!

And then I chose a different palette to complete each one of the dragons: blue (with a little complementary orange and some red), pink (spiced up with yellow and orange too), yellow with pale green, or a racy mix of red, purple, and orange. Remember, these are probably trendy teenage dragons!

The final step, as usual, is the delicate use of fine-line white gouache to decorate, highlight, and outline. Don't miss the little puffs of snorted smoke from the dragon who has the ball and his friend just above!

Experiment with inking and coloring the lineart, then create your own rendition on the opposite page!

PENCIL:

Begin by placing the tree in center stage. Give it a graceful bend to the left, roots that compensate by reaching out to the right, and a branch or two mid-trunk for the dragon to eventually grasp.

The neck of the dragon winds around the upper trunk, with his body behind and to the right. His wings create a circular embrace farther out from the tree, and where they spring from his back a "V" frames the opening branches. Notice that his tail makes a graceful loop that balances with the arch of the neck to bring the eye back, again and again, to his head.

PEN & INK:

Now that you are becoming proficient at creating beautiful dragon scales and wings, you can easily draw these in, first in pencil of course, and then go over your linework with a fine pen. Around the roots of the tree two serpents circle, with mushrooms and flowers decorating the ground. Beyond the high grasses rise row upon row of fir trees. Study how the bark of the tree is drawn to give a textured 3D effect. When all is inked, thoroughly erase the pencil lines.

GOUACHE:

You might begin the painting with the green of the grass and some of the distant trees. Over a first medium-to-light coat, paint subtle blades of grass in a less diluted shade of the first color.

Painting trees is always a delight! With the style you have seen here of suggesting rounded lines of growth on the trunk, you can use different strengths of brown to add shading and contour. A yellow glow is added to the sky.

Continue by painting the flowers, mushrooms, and snakes. The forest behind the dragon can be home to a variety of greens, some over-painted with extra strokes of the brush to make them less flat and to add texture.

The dragon himself is painted in bold, rich, medieval colors, reminiscent of the illuminations in ancient manuscripts. The same reds and blues used on the foreground snake will link these elements to the dragon and make a more harmonious painting.

And finally the white gouache highlights and details are added. Notice how the delicate lines running down the tail tip make it look almost shiny, and don't overlook the tiny points of white in the dragon's red eyes!

Experiment with inking and coloring the lineart, then create your own rendition on the opposite page!

PENCIL:

Begin with the first dragon. Position him cruising gently through the sky, his wings pulled backward a bit as he glides along, his tail perhaps languidly flapping to and fro.

There's ample room for a friend to join him. Perhaps a lady dragon!

PEN & INK:

Now that the two of them are there, the upper atmosphere can be filled in with fluffy little clouds, the details on the two dragons can be drawn in, and all the pencil work redrawn in ink.

GOUACHE:

The first painting step is a light wash over the entire scene. Having moistened the paper with a sponge or large brush, apply delicate strokes of yellow, blue, and pink, as indicated, allowing them to blend into one another.

Now dress the gentleman dragon in his scaley suit of greens, blues, and yellows, with a chic touch of pale violet. The lady (if it is a lady dragon) picks up the violet theme and combines it with darker purple, more yellow, a touch of green, and a rich golden ochre.

Here is the step for adding white detail, as well as a few strokes of other colors on both dragons.

As this is a flight through fantasy skies, let your imagination inspire your choice of pastel colors to tint the clouds, harmonizing these shades with those already present in the dragons, of course.

Experiment with inking and coloring the lineart, then create your own rendition on the opposite page!

PENCIL:

The body of this sleeping dragon is positioned in the center of the page, almost in the form of a question mark! Keep the movement from tail to snout fluid and well-rounded. Indicate the placement of the heaps of crystals using a soft pencil, so you can adjust and erase as needed.

Add the cave entrance behind the dragon, and begin to work on the body details and the curved wings. Begin "sculpting" the angles on the foreground crystals.

PEN & INK:

In pencil first, and then in ink, complete the scales, head, and feet of the dragon, and all the points and angled surfaces of the crystals piled about him. His tail, resting on the crystals, is given some turns and folds. Add the stalactites coming down from the ceiling, and the rough edges on the cave walls and entrance tunnel. Erase all pencil marks once the inking is completed and thoroughly dry.

GOUACHE:

Choose a bluish purple for the wash on the cave walls and the foreground crystals, allowing the paint to create streaks here and there, which will give the effect of reflections on the shiny surfaces of the stone.

The same technique of gouache-
wash on a moistened area is used
for the sandy cave floor, this time in
a yellow ochre.

Keep the original purple in your
palette for the amethysts, but make
at least two other nuances, using
the same color with the addition
of more blue, and elsewhere, more
red. This will unify the range of
tones, but give a good variety of
depth and intensity. Use these
colors on certain surfaces of the
crystals, and on the stalactites and
tunnel.

Now paint the dragon mostly in various shades of green, with a little purple.

And finally, with your white gouache, add the detail highlights and contours, and don't forget to whiten the vapor escaping the monster's nostrils (and maybe just the hint of a glisten under his eyelids, as he keeps a sleepy lookout for intruders).

Experiment with
inking and coloring the
lineart, then create your
own rendition on the
opposite page!

PENCIL:

In the center of your page, leaving good margins all around, position the dragon with four or five graceful curves of his long body, receding into the distance and getting progressively thinner as they go. Indicate the placement of her legs, and the general shape of the head.

Now begin to decorate the monster with underwater styles of fins and ears, a seaweed crest, webbed feet, and long fangs. Roughly add three curious fishes, a starfish, a couple of seashells, and a little waving seaweed in soft pencil.

PEN & INK:

Continue developing the scene with the addition of other fishes (one is bit of a rebel and insists on swimming in the wrong direction), shells, seaweed, and bubbles. Embellish the body details on the dragon a little further as well. (And don't overlook the lovely little crab and the seahorse!)

GOUACHE:

This gouache wash is a bit different from the others we have done. Moisten the paper as usual, and sweep across the page with a large brush using blue, green, and turquoise paint—but then immediately cover the wet paint with a piece of plastic film (just like you use in the kitchen!), and scrunch it up with your fingertips. Once it is wrinkled, leave it in place until dry. When dry, lift off the plastic film to reveal a wavering effect in the paint—perfect for this underwater scene!

Begin the painting stage by coloring the dragon, using bold and bright blues and greens, and a little pale peach as a contrast color.

Continue your painting with the orangey-red seaweed, the blue and orange fishes, and the yellows of the starfish and some of the shells. A little whitish mauve is added here and there as well.

Paint the seahorse and crab, and finish adding color to all the fishes, shells, and grasses. Overpaint with extra colors on all of these elements, to add interest and shading.

In the white-gouache stage, add all the extra details and highlights, as usual, to both the central deep-sea dragon and the other elements and characters that share her habitat. (Don't forget a little glint of white in the eyes of the crab and fishes!)

Experiment with inking and coloring the lineart, then create your own rendition on the opposite page!

PENCIL:

Begin with a single sweeping curve in the center of your page, representing the dragon's back, and then double it to create the basic body form. Add the head and indicate the placement of horns, as well as fire coming from the dragon's open mouth. Draw two lines to show the movement of the wings, one more extended, the other more bent, but both roughly at the same height.

Draw the wings. Sketch the one on the left above the initial curved line. Sketch the one on the right below the first bent line that you drew. Add detail to the dragon's head, and draw its legs and the crest along its back. Establish the horizon line, with mountains and volcanoes, and the rivers of fiery lava flowing over the land.

PEN & INK:

Complete the details of the dragon's head, body, and wings, the flames from his mouth, and his pointed claws. Draw the distant volcanoes and hills, the foreground mountain peaks, and wavy lines of lava flowing into the foreground.

MARKER:

Fill in the dragon in bright and deep greens, balanced with a little yellow and orange.

Render the volcanoes in shades of brown and fire engine red. Use a little of the same yellow and orange you used on the dragon on the volcanoes, to link these design elements together. Indicate the billows of toxic smoke with greyish blue on the edges, and yellow in the centers of the smoke clouds. The foreground mountains are, as yet, untouched by the lava, so they are colored in different shades of brown.

For the land, you may decide that some areas are still earth-colored, while others are the rivers of red, orange, or yellow lava.

In the final marker step, add secondary areas of color to those already filled in: brown on red, red on orange, orange on yellow, dark green on light green. White "correction" marker or paint marker can be used to outline some of the scales, detail the twist of the horns, and decorate the wings.

Experiment with
inking and coloring the
lineart, then create your
own rendition on the
following page!

ABOUT THE AUTHOR

Jane Sullivan is a fantasy artist, calligrapher, and Medieval-style illuminator. She drew the dragons that populate this book while working on an illuminated psalter for the Abbey of St. Martin in Ligugé, France. Her other works include guides to illuminated lettering, calligraphy, and drawing fantastical beings. Visit her online at www.calligrafee.com.

Dedicated to my dear Michel, and to Benoit and Véronique, with fond memories of dragons taking shape in Australia and in New Caledonia!